Presented to:

Never Forget The Difference You've Made

Made in the USA
Monee, IL
04 October 2022

15239514R00066